Exploring America

Written by:
Dennis J. Graham
Debra L. Hays
Pat Millie
Mimi A. Stankowich

Table of Contents

Catch the Spirit!

Test your knowledge of the American flag.

 enry, Abby, and Samantha are so excited! The mayor of their town has just announced that they're this year's winners of their town's "Catch the Spirit Contest." Every year, the honor of leading the Flag Day parade is bestowed upon the contest winners!

To the right, the children are leading this year's parade. Below the parade are the 10 contest questions about the US flag that they had to answer correctly. Answer the questions to find out if you'd have been a flag contest finalist!

Catch the Spirit Contest Quiz

1. Today's 50-Star Flag was first flown
   ○ in 1900.
   □ in 1960.

2. The colors red, white, and blue in the US flag stand for
   ○ courage, purity, and justice.
   □ life, air, and water.

3. Many historians consider the first national flag to be
   ○ the Grand Union Flag.
   □ the Flag of 1818.

4. Americans celebrate Flag Day on June 14th because that was the day on which
   ○ the official flag was adopted in 1777.
   □ the Declaration of Independence was written.

5. The stripes in the flag stand for
   ○ the number of years it took to design the flag.
   □ the first thirteen colonies.

6. The 48-Star Flag served as the national flag
   ○ after Alaska and Hawaii became states.
   □ longer than any other US flag.

7. True or False: A rattlesnake was used on many Revolutionary flags to show American defiance of the British.
   ○ True   □ False

8. One reason the flag continued to change even after it was officially adopted was
   ○ the people weren't happy with the design of the flag.
   □ the resolution didn't state how many stars and stripes could be added.

9. True or False: The Flag of 1795 had more stripes than the Flag of 1818.
   ○ True   □ False

10. The colonists wanted a new flag because
    ○ the British Flag of 1606 was getting old.
    □ they wanted a flag that would be a symbol of their independence.

The American Flag

The American flag is a symbol of independence, freedom, and democracy. We show respect for our flag in the way we display it, pledge our allegiance to it, and stand at attention whenever it's presented. The Stars and Stripes has been an important part of American history, and has an important history of its own!

The 50-Star Flag

Today's 50-Star Flag was flown for the first time on July 4, 1960, after Alaska and Hawaii became states. The Great Seal of the US states that the red stands for hardiness and courage; the white stands for purity and innocence; and the blue stands for vigilance, perseverance, and justice!

British Flag of 1606

This British flag was one of the first flags to be flown over the colonies.

Grand Union Flag

Also known as the Continental Colors, this flag was, unofficially, the first national flag of the United States.

Flag of 1777

On June 14, 1777, the Stars and Stripes became the first official national flag, making it an even stronger symbol of independence. In honor of that day, June 14th is now Flag Day!

Flag of 1795

The resolution adopting the new flag stated that the stars and stripes stood for the colonies. Since the resolution didn't state exactly how many stars and stripes could be added, the Flag of 1795 had 15 of each!

The Flag of 1818

This flag returned to 13 stripes, for the original colonies, and carried one star for each state. From this point on, as states became part of the US, only new stars were added.

Continental Jack

A number of flags, like the Continental Jack, used a rattlesnake to show American defiance of the British.

The 48-Star Flag

This flag served as the national flag the longest, from 1912 to 1959.

Answers

A Business Gone Sour...

Help a first-time travel agent get his US travel tips in order.

ike so many Americans, Oliver's big dream is to open his own business. But which business is best?

Oliver thought and thought. "Americans love to travel," he said at last. "And with so much to see and do in the United States, a travel agency is a great business to start!"

So begins the story of "Oliver's All-Over Money-Back Guarantee Travel Agency."

Oliver immediately prepared colorful brochures on exciting places to visit. Money soon began pouring in from families getting ready for their summer trips. The trouble is that Oliver's haphazard research caused some of the brochure information to be printed incorrectly. Can you figure out what's right and wrong with his brochures before another family trip starts out on the wrong foot?

Look at the 10 travel brochures Oliver has prepared for his new clients. For each brochure, decide if the information:

○ **Is correct as shown**

△ **Places the tourist spot in the wrong location**

□ **Includes the right location, but an incorrect description**

OLIVER'S "ALL-OVER" TRAVEL AGENCY

MONEY BACK GUARANTEE

THE WHITE HOUSE ⑩

Washington, DC
What's the most famous address in town? Sixteen hundred Pennsylvania Avenue — home to the President and his family, of course.

MT. RUSHMORE ④

Black Hills, SD
See the world's largest statue, featuring likenesses of Presidents Washington, Jefferson, Lincoln, and Kennedy.

THE HOLLYWOOD SIGN ③

San Diego, CA
Visit the city of glamorous movie stars, show-biz celebrities, and millionaires!

THE GOLDEN GATE BRIDGE ⑨

Portland, OR
There's no sight prettier than that of the Golden Gate Bridge rising majestically from its bed of downy-white fog.

GATEWAY ARCH ⑦

St. Louis, MO
Stand beneath this gleaming, stainless-steel monument to the Louisiana Purchase and the opening of the Western United States.

INDEPENDENCE HALL ⑥

Gettysburg, PA
Re-live history at the hall in which our Founding Fathers signed the Declaration of Independence in 1776.

STATUE OF LIBERTY ⑤

New York, NY
Tour our nation's most treasured symbol of our freedom, a gift from France in 1884.

THE SEARS TOWER ②

Chicago, IL
Get a breathtaking view from this 110-story building...the world's tallest!

THE ALAMO ⑧

San Antonio, TX
Grab your boots and cowboy hat, and c'mon down to this famous monument to the American War for Independence.

OLD NORTH CHURCH ①

Boston, MA
Visit the home of America's first Thanksgiving feast.

"Hello. You've reached Oliver's All-Over Money-Back Guarantee Travel Agency. I'm sorry we can't take your call now, but you can leave your message at the sound of the beep."

Beep...
"We just love the Sears Tower in Chicago! Its 110 stories look like 1,010! Thanks so much, Oliver."

Beep...
"We didn't see the President, but we did take the White House Tour during our stay in Washington, DC. Found it no problem."

Beep...
"Oliver, I just want you to know how much we loved the Statue of Liberty tour you booked for us. It was just as your brochure said!"

Beep...
"Oliver, we're calling from Saint Louis. The Gateway Arch is wonderful. Thanks for a great vacation."

Beep...
"Having a great vacation, Oliver, but some of the facts in your brochure need fixing!"

Beep...
"Oliver, the battle at the Alamo took place in the 1836 Texas Revolution. San Antonio's very nice, though."

Beep...
"Thought you'd like to know that the Old North Church in Boston was used to signal Paul Revere's famous ride — not for the first Thanksgiving."

Beep...
"The Black Hills are spectacular, and Mt. Rushmore is great, too. But Theodore Roosevelt's likeness is here, not John F. Kennedy's."

Beep...
"Oliver, you sent us to the wrong city! Where's our refund?"

Beep...
"What kind of travel agency do you run? San Diego's very pretty, but the Hollywood sign...it's in Los Angeles!"

Beep...
"People laughed when we asked for directions to the Golden Gate Bridge in Portland. They told us it's in San Francisco. How can we get a refund?"

Beep...
"Oliver, you gave us an address in Gettysburg, but Independence Hall really is in Philadelphia, PA. We want our money back!"

On Your Own

Call or visit your local chamber of commerce to find out about a local building or site that out-of-town visitors would like to see. Design your own travel brochure for the landmark. Include as many facts as you can find about its history and importance.

Answers

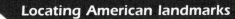

Discover America

Help two lucky game-show players explore how ten US places got their names!

Today is an exciting day for Baxter and Natasha! They've been chosen to play the famous T.V. game show, <u>Discover America</u>. Lucky for them, today's question category is "Places and Explorers," their favorite topic! If they can correctly say how ten US places were named, they will win an all-expense paid trip from coast to coast! The clock is ticking away. Can you help them before time runs out?

Look at the 10 US places on the screen to the right of Baxter and Natasha. Listed with each of the places is the name of an explorer. For each place, decide if it was:

○ **Explored by and named for the explorer**

△ **Named in honor of (but never visited by) the explorer**

☐ **Named for someone or something else**

Discover America
Places and Explorers

1. **Columbus, OH**
   Christopher Columbus (c.1451-1506)
2. **Lewiston, ID**
   Meriwether Lewis (1774-1809)
3. **Lake Champlain, NY**
   Samuel de Champlain (1567-1635)
4. **Johnstown, PA**
   John Muir (1838-1914)
5. **Balboa Park, CA**
   Vasco Nuñez de Balboa (c.1475-1519)
6. **San Francisco, CA**
   Francisco Pizarro (1475-1541)
7. **Fremont, CA**
   John Fremont (1813-1890)
8. **Pike's Peak, CO**
   Zebulon Pike (1779-1813)
9. **Hudson River, NY**
   Henry Hudson (? -1611)
10. **Drake, ND**
    Sir Francis Drake (c.1540-1596)

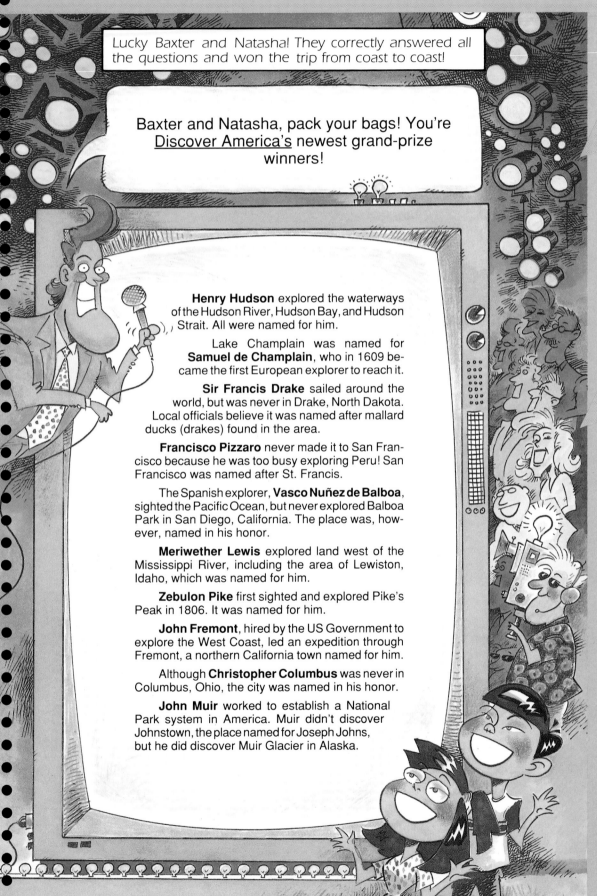

Lucky Baxter and Natasha! They correctly answered all the questions and won the trip from coast to coast!

Baxter and Natasha, pack your bags! You're <u>Discover America's</u> newest grand-prize winners!

Henry Hudson explored the waterways of the Hudson River, Hudson Bay, and Hudson Strait. All were named for him.

Lake Champlain was named for **Samuel de Champlain**, who in 1609 became the first European explorer to reach it.

Sir Francis Drake sailed around the world, but was never in Drake, North Dakota. Local officials believe it was named after mallard ducks (drakes) found in the area.

Francisco Pizzaro never made it to San Francisco because he was too busy exploring Peru! San Francisco was named after St. Francis.

The Spanish explorer, **Vasco Nuñez de Balboa**, sighted the Pacific Ocean, but never explored Balboa Park in San Diego, California. The place was, however, named in his honor.

Meriwether Lewis explored land west of the Mississippi River, including the area of Lewiston, Idaho, which was named for him.

Zebulon Pike first sighted and explored Pike's Peak in 1806. It was named for him.

John Fremont, hired by the US Government to explore the West Coast, led an expedition through Fremont, a northern California town named for him.

Although **Christopher Columbus** was never in Columbus, Ohio, the city was named in his honor.

John Muir worked to establish a National Park system in America. Muir didn't discover Johnstown, the place named for Joseph Johns, but he did discover Muir Glacier in Alaska.

On Your Own

Do some exploring of your own. Go to the library or to your city hall and find out how your town or city got its name. Was it named for an individual who actually discovered the area, a community leader, a famous person, an animal, or something else altogether?

Answers

Altered States

Can you match these mixed-up states with their well-known nicknames?

 ach of the 50 US states has its own story of how its nickname and outline shape came to be. Some states, for example, have rivers, mountain ranges, or other natural boundaries to thank for their shapes. Other boundaries follow lines of longitude or latitude.

As with state boundaries, state nicknames also have developed in several easily recognizable ways. Think of state nicknames as advertising slogans. Most states try to put their "best foot forward" in their nicknames. As a result, most nicknames describe a state's unique physical, historical, or agricultural heritage.

Look at the list of 10 state nicknames below. Then find the matching state outlines at the right. For each state outline you find, decide if it is shown:

○　　Right-side up

△　　Upside down

☐　　Tilted on its side

1. The Palmetto State

2. The Silver State

3. The Volunteer State

4. The Buckeye State

5. The Sooner State

6. The Beehive State

7. The Bay State

8. The Wolverine State

9. The Sunshine State

10. The Golden State

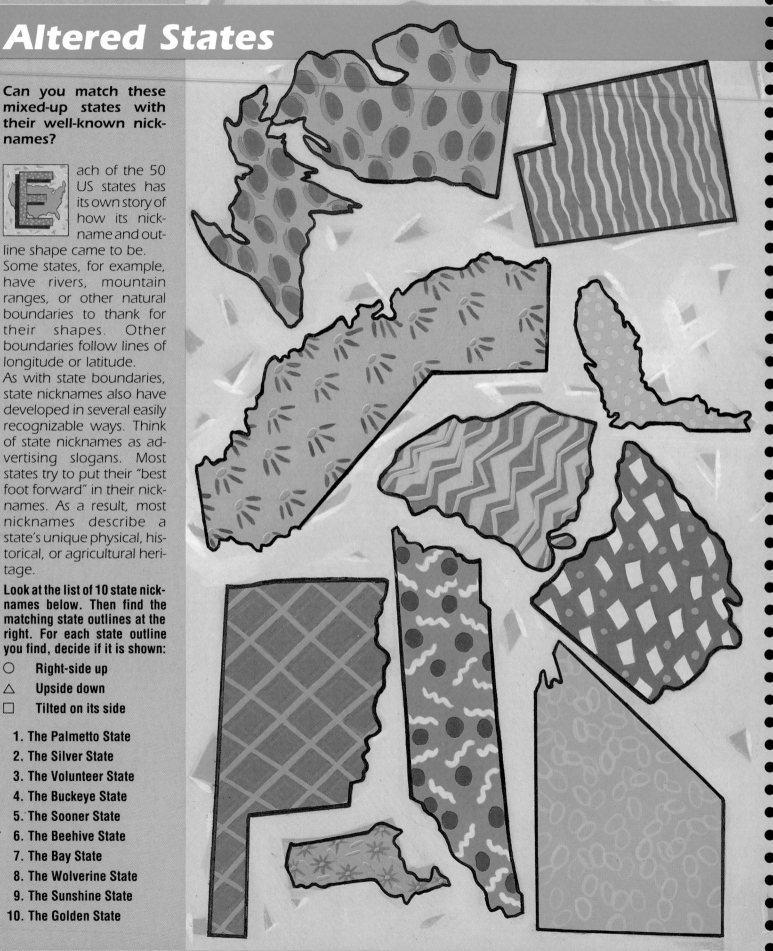

8

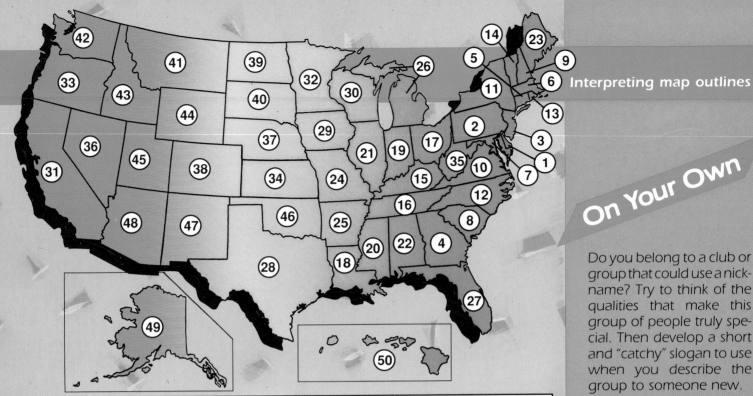

On Your Own

Do you belong to a club or group that could use a nickname? Try to think of the qualities that make this group of people truly special. Then develop a short and "catchy" slogan to use when you describe the group to someone new.

Answers

Here's a map of all 50 states showing the order each state was admitted to the Union. Below is a fact-filled guide to the states. Explore it to learn some of the ways America grew and developed pride in itself.

	STATE	CAPITAL	NICKNAME	ADMITTED
1.	Delaware	Dover	First State	1787
2.	Pennsylvania	Harrisburg	Keystone State	1787
3.	New Jersey	Trenton	Garden State	1787
4.	Georgia	Atlanta	Empire State of the South	1788
5.	Connecticut	Hartford	Constitution State	1788
6.	Massachusetts	Boston	Bay State	1788
7.	Maryland	Annapolis	Old Line State	1788
8.	South Carolina	Columbia	Palmetto State	1788
9.	New Hampshire	Concord	Granite State	1788
10.	Virginia	Richmond	Old Dominion	1788
11.	New York	Albany	Empire State	1788
12.	North Carolina	Raleigh	Tar Heel State	1789
13.	Rhode Island	Providence	Ocean State	1790
14.	Vermont	Montpelier	Green Mountain State	1791
15.	Kentucky	Frankfort	Bluegrass State	1792
16.	Tennessee	Nashville	Volunteer State	1796
17.	Ohio	Columbus	Buckeye State	1803
18.	Louisiana	Baton Rouge	Pelican State	1812
19.	Indiana	Indianapolis	Hoosier State	1816
20.	Mississippi	Jackson	Magnolia State	1817
21.	Illinois	Springfield	Land of Lincoln	1818
22.	Alabama	Montgomery	Yellowhammer State	1819
23.	Maine	Augusta	Pine Tree State	1820
24.	Missouri	Jefferson City	Show Me State	1821
25.	Arkansas	Little Rock	Land of Opportunity	1836
26.	Michigan	Lansing	Wolverine State	1837

	STATE	CAPITAL	NICKNAME	ADMITTED
27.	Florida	Tallahassee	Sunshine State	1845
28.	Texas	Austin	Lone Star State	1845
29.	Iowa	Des Moines	Hawkeye State	1846
30.	Wisconsin	Madison	Badger State	1848
31.	California	Sacramento	Golden State	1850
32.	Minnesota	St. Paul	Gopher State	1858
33.	Oregon	Salem	Beaver State	1859
34.	Kansas	Topeka	Sunflower State	1861
35.	West Virginia	Charleston	Mountain State	1863
36.	Nevada	Carson City	Silver State	1864
37.	Nebraska	Lincoln	Cornhusker State	1867
38.	Colorado	Denver	Centennial State	1876
39.	North Dakota	Bismarck	Flickertail State	1889
40.	South Dakota	Pierre	Land of Infinite Variety	1889
41.	Montana	Helena	Treasure State	1889
42.	Washington	Olympia	Evergreen State	1889
43.	Idaho	Boise	Gem State	1890
44.	Wyoming	Cheyenne	Equality State	1890
45.	Utah	Salt Lake City	Beehive State	1896
46.	Oklahoma	Oklahoma City	Sooner State	1907
47.	New Mexico	Santa Fe	Land of Enchantment	1912
48.	Arizona	Phoenix	Grand Canyon State	1912
49.	Alaska	Juneau	Last Frontier	1959
50.	Hawaii	Honolulu	Aloha State	1959

Fantastic Festivals

Find out just where in the US these fun-filled festivals can be found.

Carmen, Andy, and Jennifer always complain about the food in their school cafeteria. Now they're getting their just desserts — their principal has given them a special assignment. They're to check out food festivals throughout the country to find new and interesting recipes for the cafeteria to cook up. The three food finders have each put together a list of festivals to visit, but are not exactly sure where each one is held.

Can you help Carmen, Andy, and Jennifer discover the state where each festival is held?

Choose the correct location for each of the 10 festivals listed on the right.

1. ○ Texas ☐ Hawaii
2. ○ California
   ☐ Vermont
3. ○ Massachusetts
   ☐ Louisiana
4. ○ Alaska
   ☐ West Virginia
5. ○ Florida
   ☐ South Dakota
6. ○ Oklahoma
   ☐ Massachusetts
7. ○ Louisiana
   ☐ Vermont
8. ○ Missouri
   ☐ Hawaii
9. ○ West Virginia
   ☐ Nevada
10. ○ Arizona ☐ Missouri

PRINCIPAL

JENNIFER

SPICE OF LIFE FESTIVALS

1. Prairie Dog Chili Cook-Off and World Championship of Pickled Quail Egg Eating
2. Gilroy Garlic Festival
3. Jambalaya Festival and Art Show
4. Great Sitka Herring Festival

Andy

SWEET TOOTH FESTIVALS

5. Citrus Festival
6. Cranberry Harvest Festival
7. Maple Sugar Festival

Carmen

Health Nut FESTIVALS

8. Macadamia Nut Harvest Festival
9. Preston County Buckwheat Festival
10. Mexico Jaycee Soybean Festival

Paul's a good guy, but unfortunately, he lost the election! Although he didn't prove to be much of a speech maker, the club members were so impressed by the campaign slogans in Paul's speech that they voted him club historian! What did he put on the first page of the historian's scrapbook? You guessed it . . . campaign slogans used during US presidential elections!

William Henry Harrison
9th president (1841)
"Tippecanoe and Tyler, too"

James K. Polk
11th president (1845-1849)
"54-40 or Fight!"

Andrew Jackson
7th president (1829-1837)
"Let the people rule."

Abraham Lincoln
16th president (1861-1865)
"A house divided against itself cannot stand."

William McKinley
25th president (1897-1901)
"A full dinner pail"

Theodore Roosevelt
26th president (1901-1909)
"Square deal"

Warren G. Harding
29th president (1921-1923)
"A return to normalcy"

Herbert Hoover
31st president (1929-1933)
"A chicken in every pot"

Harry Truman
33rd president (1945-1953)
"The buck stops here."

John F. Kennedy
35th president (1961-1963)
"The New Frontier"

On Your Own

Slogans not only represent the ideas that candidates believe in, but are also easy to remember and tend to stick in people's mind. Create a slogan about something you really believe in. Make a campaign button. Now, write your slogan on the button and wear it!

Answers

Happy Trails

Locate towns with unusual names on a highway map of Texas.

 owboy Tex has decided to take a rest from his life of ropin' and ridin'. He's going to visit as many of his old cowboy pals as he can.

To plan his trip, Tex put a big map of Texas on his wall. Then he wrote in all the names of the towns in which his friends live. Next, Tex drew in the roads he'll take as he drives around the state. Now, all he has to do to figure out who he'll visit is to match the towns his friends live in to the highways he'll be driving.

Help Tex plan his vacation. For each highway given, decide which town he can visit on that highway.

1. 126
   ○ Shiner ☐ Noodle

2. 40
   ○ Shamrock
   ☐ Sulphur Springs

3. 303
   ○ Sunrise ☐ Sundown

4. 59
   ○ Turkey ☐ Beeville

5. 90
   ○ Paradise ☐ Valentine

6. 137
   ○ Punkin Center
   ☐ Pumkin

7. 67
   ○ Blanket ☐ Comfort

8. 380
   ○ Notrees ☐ Old Glory

9. 281
   ○ Twin Sisters
   ☐ Seven Sisters

10. 35
    ○ N. Zulch ☐ Old Ocean

TEXAS

Highway Types

- U.S. Interstate
- U.S. Federal
- State
- State Secondary or County

Sunray · · Shamrock · Dawn · Turkey · Sundown · Old Glory · Punkin Center · Loving · Notrees · Noodle · Blanket · Sunset · Paradise · Sulphur Springs · Texon · Early · Eden · Sunrise · Quicksand · N. Zulch · Pumkin · Best · Comfort · Valentine · Marathon · Twin Sisters · Shiner · Old Ocean · Bigfoot · Beeville · Seven Sisters

Even after starting his trip, Cowboy Tex is _still_ confused

"Well, y'all can't get to Dawn from here, but you can get to Sundown if you take 303. To reach Noodle, drive down 126. Just north of there you can get to Old Glory if you take 380. Now, I've heard that Interstate 40 is a quick way to drive to Shamrock, but Punkin Center isn't on that road—it's down 137.

"I'd drive down 281 to Twin Sisters. I went to school with twin sisters—never could tell 'em apart. Anyway, take 35 to Old Ocean. 67 will get you to Blanket and 59 will land you in Beeville. You should find Valentine on 90, but I'm afraid you won't find Paradise. Y'all come back now!"

On Your Own

Would you like to name a place in the US? First, find a peak with no name on a US Geological Survey topographical map. Then send your suggested name to:

Executive Secretary of Domestic Geographical Names
U.S. Geological Survey
National Center
Mail Stop 523
12201 Sunrise Valley Drive
Reston, VA 22092

Answers

Terrific Tales

Get ready for some stirring stories about deeds of daring!

 t's campfire time at Indian Springs Camp, and the campers have gathered round the fire for a once-a-year treat. Their counselor, Harvey, has promised to tell them ten tales about American folk characters. The only problem is, Harvey hasn't told his tales since last summer. Now he's having trouble remembering which object or event goes with each folk character. Can you help Harvey remember the details that go with each story?

Match each of the objects or events in the boxes on the right with the 10 folk characters listed below.

1. **Nellie Bly**
   ○ A   ☐ D

2. **Paul Bunyan**
   ○ B   ☐ C

3. **Ichabod Crane**
   ○ J   ☐ F

4. **Pocahontas**
   ○ G   ☐ I

5. **John Henry**
   ○ H   ☐ B

6. **Johnny Appleseed**
   ○ D   ☐ E

7. **Buffalo Bill**
   ○ H   ☐ J

8. **Uncle Remus**
   ○ H   ☐ E

9. **Betsy Ross**
   ○ D   ☐ I

10. **Casey Jones**
    ○ H   ☐ G

Long,
long
ago . . .

A. Reporter's notebook	B. Hammer	C. Babe the Blue Ox	D. Apple tree	E. Brer Rabbit
F. Headless Horseman	G. Saved John Smith	H. Engineer's cap	I. American flag	J. Wild West Show poster

You've saved the night and Harvey's reputation as a great storyteller! Now the happy campers are off to bed, ready to dream of heroic deeds!

My favorite story is either the one about Paul Bunyan and his ox or the one about Ichabod Crane and that creepy Headless Horseman.

I think Pocahontas was pretty brave to save John Smith. And so was Nellie Bly when she traveled the world as a reporter.

It sure was great that Johnny Appleseed planted all those orchards – although it would have been neat to make a US flag like Betsy Ross did!

The funniest story was the one Uncle Remus tells about Brer Rabbit. But the most exciting story told how John Henry used his hammer in the race against the steam drill.

I'd like to star in a Wild West Show as Buffalo Bill did, or be a heroic train engineer like Casey Jones.

On Your Own

Try some storytelling yourself. Find a story about a folk character you like. Read the story enough times so you're familiar with the details. Then tell the story in your own words. When you've practiced a few times, you'll be ready to try out your storytelling skills on your family.

Answers

American Indian Artifacts

Eagle-eye this trading post window display to see which objects have disappeared.

Il morning, photographers from <u>Trading Post Times</u> have been working very hard. They've created a special display of American Indian artifacts to appear on next month's cover.

Then the photographers made a big mistake — they took a lunch break! During lunch, Maddie, the cleaning lady, decided the display needed just a bit of "sprucing up." She thought the arrangement looked too untidy, so she moved things around to organize them. She's also removed some of the artifacts and put in some others instead.

Look at the two arrangements of artifacts at the right. The top picture shows the display the photographers created. The bottom picture shows the effects of Maddie's "sprucing up." Decide which of the 10 artifacts in the photographer's display are still in Maddie's arrangement, and which have been removed.

○ Object is still in display

☐ Object has been removed from display

1. Kickapoo prayer stick
2. Cheyenne saddle
3. Hopi Kachina mask
4. Navaho sand painting
5. Pomo feather basket
6. Iroquois wampum belt
7. Chilkat blanket
8. Haida totem pole
9. Interior Salish bow
10. Havasupai water vessel

Bows and arrows were the most common Indian weapon, and were vital for tribes who hunted.

Totem poles showed the titles or lineages of the heads of the households, or were carved with symbols associated with the tribe or clan.

Wampum beads were carved from whelk and clam shells. The tiny purple and white beads were woven into belts given in friendship or with treaties. Wampum was so valuable it was even used for money.

The markings on prayer sticks showed the order of past events or of prayers used during ceremonies.

As part of their religious duties, masked Kachina dancers visited the homes of children to ask if they had been behaving well. Children who had not behaved were punished.

Northwest tribes measured wealth by the amount of blankets, copper shields, and canoes a person owned.

Whew! The photographers managed to find all the missing items and fix the display just in time! As you can see, the magazine layout is a great success.

Navaho sand paintings made from sand, seeds, and minerals were important parts of healing ceremonies.

The Pomo Indians were among the finest basket makers in the New World. They often combined beads, shells, and feathers in ceremonial baskets like this one.

Havasupai baskets coated with pitch (resin or tar) were woven so tightly they could hold water.

Horses brought to the Americas by the Spanish changed the life of Plains Indians who could now follow the buffalo herds over long distances.

Eastern Woodlands

Plains

Northwest Coast

California

Intermountain

Southwest

On Your Own

Make your own sand painting. Mix some clean white sand with a few drops of food coloring. Paint a thin layer of white glue over all areas you want to be a particular color. Sprinkle sand on the glued area and wait for the glue to dry before you move on to the next color.

Answers

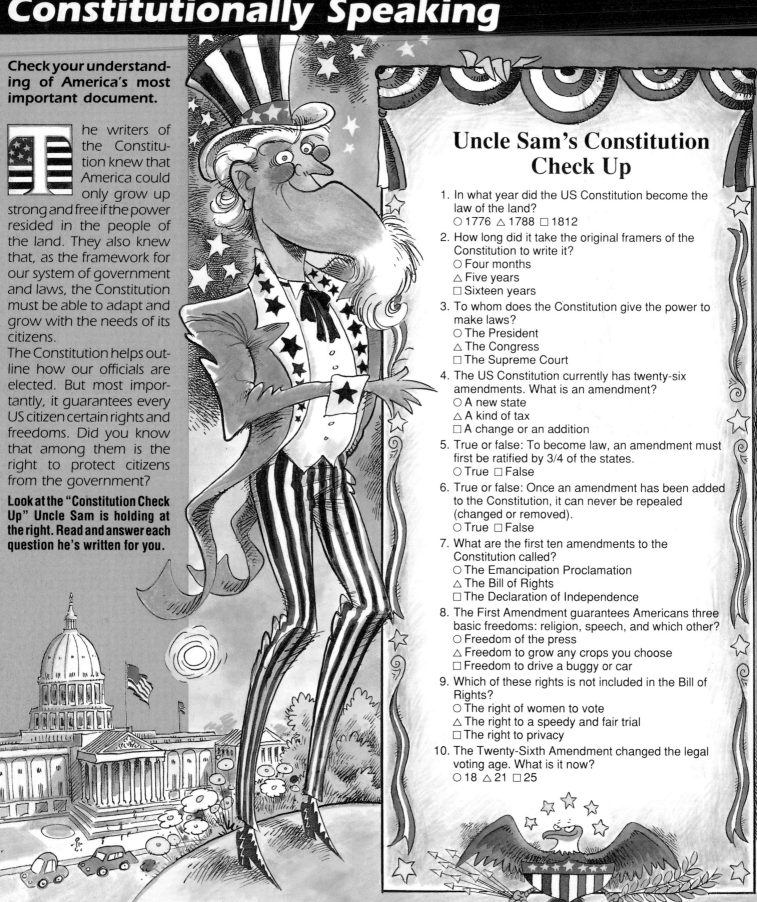

Check your understanding of America's most important document.

The writers of the Constitution knew that America could only grow up strong and free if the power resided in the people of the land. They also knew that, as the framework for our system of government and laws, the Constitution must be able to adapt and grow with the needs of its citizens.

The Constitution helps outline how our officials are elected. But most importantly, it guarantees every US citizen certain rights and freedoms. Did you know that among them is the right to protect citizens from the government?

Look at the "Constitution Check Up" Uncle Sam is holding at the right. Read and answer each question he's written for you.

Uncle Sam's Constitution Check Up

1. In what year did the US Constitution become the law of the land?
   ○ 1776 △ 1788 □ 1812

2. How long did it take the original framers of the Constitution to write it?
   ○ Four months
   △ Five years
   □ Sixteen years

3. To whom does the Constitution give the power to make laws?
   ○ The President
   △ The Congress
   □ The Supreme Court

4. The US Constitution currently has twenty-six amendments. What is an amendment?
   ○ A new state
   △ A kind of tax
   □ A change or an addition

5. True or false: To become law, an amendment must first be ratified by 3/4 of the states.
   ○ True □ False

6. True or false: Once an amendment has been added to the Constitution, it can never be repealed (changed or removed).
   ○ True □ False

7. What are the first ten amendments to the Constitution called?
   ○ The Emancipation Proclamation
   △ The Bill of Rights
   □ The Declaration of Independence

8. The First Amendment guarantees Americans three basic freedoms: religion, speech, and which other?
   ○ Freedom of the press
   △ Freedom to grow any crops you choose
   □ Freedom to drive a buggy or car

9. Which of these rights is not included in the Bill of Rights?
   ○ The right of women to vote
   △ The right to a speedy and fair trial
   □ The right to privacy

10. The Twenty-Sixth Amendment changed the legal voting age. What is it now?
    ○ 18 △ 21 □ 25

Uncle Sam wants you to know your rights and cherish the Constitution that gives you those rights! Here are some important facts to remember.

The Constitution is made up of the Preamble, the Articles, and the Amendments. The Preamble is the introduction to the Constitution. Articles I through VII come next. The first three articles list a set of rules for forming a government. The Founding Fathers decided that there would be three branches of government — Congress, the President, and the Supreme Court. Congress has the authority to make the laws, the President must make sure the laws are obeyed, and the Supreme Court helps explain the law.

Article IV lists a set of rules for the states to follow. Article V gives the people the right to change or amend the Constitution. But three-fourths of the states must approve the amendment before it becomes the law. Article VI states that the Constitution shall be "the supreme law of the land." And Article VII states that before the Constitution could become law, nine of the thirteen states had to ratify, or accept it. On June 21, 1788, the Constitution, consisting of the Preamble and the Articles, became the law of the land.

An amendment is a change or addition to the Constitution. The first ten amendments are called the Bill of Rights. These amendments were ratified in 1791, after the Constitution became law. The Bill of Rights outlined personal rights and freedoms. For example, the First Amendment guarantees freedom of religion, of speech, and of the press. The Fourth Amendment guarantees the right to privacy. The Sixth Amendment guarantees the right to a speedy, fair trial. And the Ninth Amendment says that the people can have more rights than those listed in the Constitution!

Sixteen new amendments have been written since the Bill of Rights. These amendments added new laws, guaranteed new rights and freedoms, and changed some laws. For example, in Amendment Nineteen, women were finally given the right to vote. Amendment Twenty-six changed the voting age to eighteen. And Amendment Twenty-one repealed (reversed) the Eighteenth Amendment!

The Constitution of the United States of America stands for the nation and all the people who make it up. Abraham Lincoln said, ". . .government of the people, by the people and for the people, shall not perish from the earth." It took the writers of the Constitution only four months to write a Constitution that has lasted longer and worked better than any other in history!

AMERICAN HISTORY

On Your Own

You can send for a replica of the Constitution for $2.00 or send for a free catalog called "Documents From America's Past" by writing to:

National Archives and Records Service
General Services Administration
Washington, DC 20408

Answers

Speaking with "Forked" Tongues

Americans speak English, right? Or do they? Just listen to the jive in this All-American diner!

Words and phrases we use informally as figures of speech are called slang words and expressions. Slang can add a great deal of color to our everyday language use. Almost everyone uses slang at least some of the time. Some groups, such as waitresses or truck drivers, have developed such extensive slang vocabularies that it sometimes seems as if they're speaking a different language!

Look at the underlined expression in each conversation being held around this All-American Diner. Find the slang equivalent for each of the 10 underlined expressions in the jukeboxes at the bottom of the scene. Choose ◯, △, or ☐.

3. Don't get so steamed! It's only a <u>minor accident</u>.

10. I was <u>laughing uncontrollably</u> over the movie!

8. What state was it you said you <u>live in</u>?

7. I think I'll skip the main course and <u>go directly</u> to the dessert.

1. I'll have the meat loaf with a side of <u>potatoes</u>.

5. I want the whole place <u>neat and organized</u> when you're finished.

6. Some days I'm just a <u>clumsy person</u>.

2. That'll be <u>twenty-five cents</u> for the soda.

9. Let's go cruising in Johnny's new <u>high-powered</u> hot rod!

4. Stop <u>pretending to be asleep</u> and eat your vegetables.

△ JUKEBOX
ace in the hole
fender bender
barney clapper
bull in a china shop
horse sense
hail from
passing muster
discombobulated

◯ JUKEBOX
greased wheel
playing possum
baby kisser
two bits
out in left field
make a beeline
gobbledygook
off-beat

☐ JUKEBOX
snow job
spuds
in apple-pie order
lallygag
in stitches
blue in the face
(a) sawbuck
souped-up

How's your "slang I.Q.?" Check this Dictionary of Slang to get in on the conversations held at the All-American Diner.

All-American Diner

ace in the hole
a secret or surprise advantage

apple-pie order
neat and organized

baby kisser
politician (from their habit of kissing babies during a campaign)

barney clapper
spoiled milk

bull in a china shop
a clumsy or rough person

blue in the face
intensely angry

discombobulated
confused or upset

fender bender
a minor auto accident

gobbledygook
nonsense

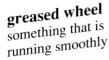

greased wheel
something that is running smoothly

hail from
to come from or live in

horse sense
common good sense

in stitches
laughing uncontrollably

lallygag
to dawdle or waste time

make a beeline
go in a straight line or manner

off-beat
unusual or unexpected

out in left field
far from the right answer

passing muster
being good enough, passing the test

playing possum
pretending to be asleep

sawbuck
a ten-dollar bill

snow job
insincere or exaggerated speech

souped-up
high-powered and fast

spuds
potatoes

two bits
twenty-five cents, a quarter

On Your Own

What slang expressions do you and your friends use? Make a "Dictionary of Slang" that defines each word or expression in a way that your parents would understand. Ask your parents to make a list of words they used when they were young, too.

Answers

Weather or Not?

Will today's weather bring rain or snow? Better re-check these forecasts to find out.

eporting the weather can be difficult. Often, the weather maps are filled with all kinds of confusing details and symbols. Look at the weather map of the US on the television screen to the right. Below the map are Sonny and Misty. Their class is visiting the TV news studio. Sonny and Misty have been asked to pretend they are weather reporters. They are trying to explain the weather map to their classmates. How accurate are their weather reports? Hint: The weather map shows the day's high temperatures in both Fahrenheit and Celsius. Example:

68/20
Fahrenheit   Celsius

For each number, read the statements of both Sonny and Misty. Compare their statements to the weather map. Decide whether:

○ **Sonny is correct**

△ **Misty is correct**

☐ **Neither is correct**

	Sonny's Report	Misty's Report
1.	There are thunderstorms in Texas today.	It is sunny and fair in Texas today.
2.	Southern Florida is experiencing warm weather.	Southern Florida is very cold—it's only 33° C today!
3.	The hottest place in the country is Honolulu, Hawaii.	The hottest place in the country is Los Angeles, California.
4.	Snowstorms have been reported in the northern Rockies.	Snowstorms have been reported in the northern Appalachians.
5.	There is a cold front over the Mississippi River Valley.	A cold front is moving into the states along the Atlantic coast.
6.	No rain activity has been reported in California.	Some rain activity has been reported in northern California.
7.	Chicago is warmer than New York City today.	New York City is warmer than Dallas, Texas today.
8.	Ohio will continue experiencing heavy rainfall and thunderstorms.	Iowa can expect thunderstorm activity throughout the day.
9.	It's fair and sunny throughout the Pacific Northwest.	It's fair and sunny throughout New England.
10.	And it is warmer today in southeastern Alaska than it is in the Denver area!	Finally, southeastern Alaska today has temperatures higher than those for the Chicago area!

The daily newspaper also carries a national weather report. Perhaps Sonny and Misty should check this evening's paper to see how they can improve their weather reporting skills!

NATIONAL WEATHER SUMMARY

Spring hasn't quite arrived in northern Alaska where snow and low temperatures were reported today. Southeastern Alaska, however, was clear and reported warmer temperatures than Denver. Snow was also reported today in the northern Rockies. Rain fell in the western areas of the Pacific Northwest and in northern California. Fair weather continued in most of the Great Plains with clear skies from the Dakotas south to Texas. Thunderstorms brought rain to Ohio. A cold front moving into the Atlantic coast states may bring rain in the next day or two, but today was sunny in New England and in coastal areas south to Florida.

TEMPERATURES AROUND THE US
High temperature for the day:

	FAHRENHEIT	CELSIUS
Chicago, IL	59	15
Dallas, TX	68	20
Denver, CO	32	0
Duluth, MN	41	5
Fairbanks, AK	12	-11
Juneau, AK	52	11
Honolulu, HI	84	29
Los Angeles, CA	76	24
Miami, FL	92	33
New York, NY	61	16
Phoenix, AZ	99*	37

*Highest temperature in nation

On Your Own

Cut out the weather map from the newspaper every day for a week. Staple the maps together to make a book. Make the cold and warm fronts on the maps "move" by flipping the pages quickly. How far do the fronts move in a week?

Answers

America a la Mode

Help organize this pageant of historical costumes.

What a show! The U.S. history pageant at Garfield school is ready to begin. The kids in the pageant are wearing clothing styles that Americans wore at different periods in history.

In their excitement, the kids have forgotten the order of their appearance on stage. The costume from furthest back in history should come out on stage first. The costume from the next period in history should follow. The line continues in this same way until the most recent clothing style comes out on stage last.

Help the kids figure out the order of their appearance before the curtain rises. Look at the 10 costumes the kids are wearing. Put the costumes in the order in which they should appear on stage.

1. First
   ○ D   □ I
2. Second
   ○ E   □ J
3. Third
   ○ F   □ H
4. Fourth
   ○ B   □ F
5. Fifth
   ○ C   □ J
6. Sixth
   ○ G   □ E
7. Seventh
   ○ H   □ F
8. Eighth
   ○ G   □ A
9. Ninth
   ○ E   □ C
10. Tenth
    ○ D   □ A

The pageant is over and the costumes have been carefully packed into boxes. Each box has been labeled with its correct historical information.

On Your Own

What styles of clothing do you think people will be wearing in the future? Design a futuristic costume kids might wear to school 100 years from now!

Answers

Colonist

Late 1700s: In the early US days, men wore wigs for special occasions. Over the wigs they wore three-cornered hats.

Civil War Era Belle

1860s: The bell-shaped dresses of this era had cagelike frames of stiff wire or bone worn underneath.

Pilgrim

1620s: Because of their religious beliefs, the Pilgrims wore modest colors and simple clothing.

Pony-tailed Teenager

1950s: Full skirts whirled when teenagers danced to rock 'n' roll, the new music sensation.

Flapper

1920s: Women were wearing short dresses for the first time! They also wore short, or "bobbed," hairstyles.

Gibson Girl

1890s: Charles Dana Gibson started a new fashion when his drawings of the attractive, athletic "Gibson Girl" appeared.

WWI Flying Ace

1917-1918: People were amazed at the skill and daring of pilots in the early days of flying. The pilots needed warm clothing and scarves to keep warm in the open cockpits!

Spanish Explorer

1500s: Spanish expeditions first explored southern areas of what is now the US. Spanish soldiers in the expeditions typically wore armored vests or shirts.

Prospector

1849: Most of the miners panning for gold were poor, but they hoped to strike it rich in the California Gold Rush.

Present-Day Kid

Late 20th Century: If you're skateboarding, comfortable clothes are jammin'.

The Grand Tour

Discover the spectacular sights to be seen at each of these magnificent national parks!

his page shows some national park photos taken by Jeremy, a young backpacker. Starting on January 1, he visited ten spectacular parks, taking a photo of a special feature he saw at each one. On each photo Jeremy wrote the name of the state he was in and the dates of his visit. To be complete, though, he should have added the names of the parks on the photos. Now he needs help remembering which fantastic park was which. Can you help him?

Check the dates to find the order in which Jeremy took his 10 photos. Then look at the 10 questions below and decide which park each photo shows.

1. ○ Bryce Canyon
   ☐ Glacier
2. ○ Isle Royale
   ☐ Yellowstone
3. ○ Everglades
   ☐ Glacier
4. ○ Yosemite
   ☐ Carlsbad Caverns
5. ○ Volcanos
   ☐ Mesa Verde
6. ○ Grand Canyon
   ☐ Isle Royale
7. ○ Everglades
   ☐ Yosemite
8. ○ Bryce Canyon
   ☐ Volcanos
9. ○ Mesa Verde
   ☐ Everglades
10. ○ Yellowstone
    ☐ Glacier

NEW MEXICO April 2 to April 7

COLORADO July 14 to July 19

MONTANA Jan. 1 to Jan. 6

FLORIDA Feb. 15 to March 5

WYOMING August 3 to Spt. 1

CALIFORNIA May 29 to June 4

ARIZONA May 3 to May 13

HAWAII April 15 to April 24

UTAH June 12 to June 26

MICHIGAN Jan. 23 to Jan. 25

Ellen J. Dreckes

Jeremy has all his facts straight. He's gluing his photos under each entry in his journal to make a travel scrapbook to show his friends and family back home. Now he's ready for next year's trip — around the world!

April 24
Could have spent the whole day watching molten lava spouting from Kilauea volcano on the island of Hawaii!

June 2
Hiked around the spectacularly shaped and colored rock formations that have been carved by the desert winds of Bryce Canyon National Park.

July 16
Spent the day exploring cliff dwellings built by the Anasazi Indians who lived on Mesa Verde from A.D. 500 to A.D. 1200.

January 24
Saw my first moose today! The island game preserve of Isle Royale National Park is home to one of the largest herds of moose in the US!

January 3
What a way to start a trip! Grinnell Glacier Crevasse (a split in the surface of a glacier) is just one of the spectacular sights in Glacier National Park.

May 3
About 120 kinds of animals live in Grand Canyon National Park. These include mountain lions, mule deer, and several animals that live nowhere else, such as the pink Grand Canyon rattlesnake.

February 15
Alligators are just some of the incredible wildlife found in the subtropical swamps of Everglades National Park.

August 10
Had to get a shot of Old Faithful since it's the most famous geyser in Yellowstone. Had to wait a while, however. Earthquake activity has made it erupt less regularly in recent years.

April 4
Sure am impressed by the limestone stalagmites and stalactites in Carlsbad Caverns!

June 1
Hiked the trail to the top of Yosemite Falls today! What a sight! The park has the largest group of freeleaping waterfalls, such as Yosemite Falls, in the world.

On Your Own

Make your own travel scrapbook. Take a large notebook along on your next trip. Record your thoughts about the things you see each day. Leave room on each journal page to glue in a photo or to make a drawing of what you saw.

Answers

An All-Round Apple-Pie Quiz

Test your knowledge about the United States with these tasty slices of American pie!

What could be more American than Mom and apple pie? Well, we've dished-up a special All-American I.Q. test to find out. Be careful, though, some of the forty statements on these pages are true, but there's definitely something hard to swallow about the others. Can you figure out which statements make sense and which are only half-baked?

Look at each statement shown on these pages. Read each statement and decide if it is:

○ True
□ False

1. The continental US is wider than the moon.
2. In the US, water flows counterclockwise down the drain.
3. America's famous cracked Liberty Bell was made by Paul Revere, the patriot and silversmith.
4. Baseball is the officially designated National Sport of the US.
5. Except for the penny, all faces on US coins point in the same direction.
6. On average, it snows more in Minneapolis, MN than in Arizona's Grand Canyon.
7. By 1800, America already had more than 100 public libraries.
8. The Statue of Liberty faces France.
9. The University of Washington is America's oldest university.
10. There is a six-foot high monument dedicated to Popeye (the cartoon character) in Crystal City, TX.

1. In 1924 Americans could buy a new Ford automobile for $265.
2. The Revolutionary War began in 1776.
3. Thomas Jefferson was America's first Postmaster General.
4. It is illegal to hunt camels in Arizona.
5. George Washington is buried in the base of the Washington Monument.
6. There once was a state called Franklin.
7. On a clear day, it's possible to see five different states from the observation deck of the Empire State Building: NJ, NY, CT, PA, and MA.
8. "E Pluribus Unum" is the official motto of the US.
9. Maine is the only US state whose name contains only one syllable.
10. Strange as it may seem, the US has never had a bald president.

Answers

Answers

1. More males than females live in the United States.
2. New York City is closer to Caracas, Venezuela than it is to Los Angeles, CA.
3. In Washington, DC, no building may be built taller than the capitol.
4. America purchased Alaska from Canada in 1867.
5. Francis Scott Key wrote "The Star Spangled Banner" during the Civil War.
6. President Truman's middle name was S — that's all!
7. It is illegal to whistle "Dixie" (the song) in US Government buildings.
8. Texas was once a country of its own and was called the Lone Star Republic.
9. The US imports more coal than it produces.
10. Congressional candidates must attend the Electoral College before holding office.

1. The Declaration of Independence wasn't signed on July 4, 1776. The actual date was July 8.
2. Hawaii is the westernmost state in the US.
3. Pennsylvania was the first US state to allow women to vote.
4. Napoleon Bonaparte never visited the United States.
5. On average, Salt Lake City, UT receives more annual snowfall than Fairbanks, AK.
6. In his day, Abraham Lincoln was the tallest man in the US.
7. George Washington wore the first plastic dentures in America.
8. Florida is the southernmost US state.
9. During the American Revolution, more colonists fought for the British than for the Continental Army.
10. In Alaska, it is illegal to look at a moose from the window of an airplane in flight.

On Your Own

Create your own All-American Apple-Pie I.Q. Quiz to play with your friends and family. Look through encyclopedias, almanacs, history books, and magazines for fascinating facts and fibs to stump the players.

Answers

A Note to Our Readers
Have you enjoyed using this *Brainbooster* book and the Decoder? We'd love to hear from you! Please write us with your comments and suggestions for additional *Brainbooster* titles you'd like to see. Our address is:

Educational Insights
Attn: Brainbooster Writers
19560 S. Rancho Way
Dominguez Hills,
CA 90220
USA